HEARTPOWER!
LEVEL 3–5SM

D1036655

WHO INVENTED RUNNING?

American Heart Association℠

HEARTPOWER! is the American Heart Association's Schoolsite Program for teaching about the heart and how to keep it healthy for a lifetime. HeartPower! Kits are available for Pre-K, Pre-K–Grade 1 Spanish Edition, Kindergarten–Grade 2, Grades 3–5, and Grades 6–8. Additional HeartPower! Kits and their components can be ordered by calling **1-800-AHA-USA1** (1-800-242-8721).

The Level 3–5 HeartPower! Kit includes:
- HeartPower! Teacher Resource Book
- HeartPower! Readers *Who Invented Running?*
- HeartPower! Video *HeartPower! Game Show*
- HeartPower! Classroom Posters
- Stethoscopes and Alcohol Swabs

Conceptual and Creative Development: Design Five, Leanna Landsmann, Inc., and Northdale Communications, Inc.

Writing and Editing: Creative Services Associates, Inc., and Nancy-Jo Hereford

Illustrations: Franklin Hammond: *No Ifs, Ands or Butts*; Kevin Hawkes: *Smoking in the Cellar*; Andy Levine: *The Spratt Family*; Roberta Ludlow: *It Is So Still*; Ainslie MacLeod: *Food Fight!*; Susan Pietrobono: *Snack Attack!*; Chris Raschka: *Why Should I Exercise?*; Fred Schrier: *Who Invented Running?* and cover; Susan Swan: *What Is the Heart?*. **Photography:** Richard Hutchings: *Fit for Fun*.

Grateful acknowledgment is made to the following for permission to reprint the copyrighted material listed below:
"It Is So Still" from *My Parents Think I'm Sleeping* by Jack Prelutsky. Copyright © 1985 by Jack Prelutsky. By permission of Greenwillow Books, a division of William Morrow & Co., Inc.
"What Is the Heart?" from *Heartbeats: Your Body, Your Heart* by Dr. Alvin & Virginia B. Silverstein.
"The Spratt Family" from *Nursery Rhymes: The Equal Rhymes Amendment* by Father Gander. Reprinted with permission of Advocacy Press from *Father Gander Nursery Rhymes*. Copyright Girls Incorporated of Greater Santa Barbara.
"Food Fight!" from *Jack and Jill,* copyright © 1994 by the Children's Better Health Institute, Benjamin Franklin Literary & Medical Society, Inc., Indianapolis, Indiana. Used by permission.
"Snack Attack!" Reprinted by special permission from Weekly Reader Corporation. *Current Health®* is published and copyrighted by Weekly Reader Corporation. All rights reserved.

"Fit for Fun." Reprinted by special permission from Weekly Reader Corporation. *Current Health®* is published and copyrighted by Weekly Reader Corporation. All rights reserved.
"Why Should I Exercise?" from *Fun with Fitness* by Alison Jane Roberts. Copyright © 1987 Hayes Publishing Ltd.
"Who Invented Running?" by Pete Garvey. Reprinted by permission of the author.
"No Ifs, Ands or Butts." Copyright © 1994 Children's Television Workshop (New York, New York). All rights reserved.
"Smoking in the Cellar" from *Rolling Harvey Down the Hill* by Jack Prelutsky. Copyright © 1980 by Jack Prelutsky. By permission of Greenwillow Books, a division of William Morrow & Co., Inc.

The American Heart Association thanks its volunteers for their input and support.

Your contributions to the American Heart Association from events such as *Jump Rope For Heart* and *Hoops For Heart* support research that helps make educational materials like this possible. For information, call **1-800-AHA-USA1** (1-800-242-8721), or online at **http://www.americanheart.org**.

ISBN 0-87493-305-6

© 1996, American Heart Association.

Manufactured in the United States of America.

You Can Have a Healthy Heart

You can have a healthy heart,

It's as easy as 1, 2, 3!

Eat healthy stuff,

Move around enough,

Live tobacco-free!

HEARTPOWER!
SM

It Is So Still

by Jack Prelutsky

It is so still, so still tonight,
there is no sound at all,
no tapping on a windowpane,
no footsteps in the hall,

no barking dog or screeching cat,
no mouse beneath my bed,
no rustle of a windy leaf,
no raindrops overhead.

I lie beneath my covers
with my pillow to my ear,
and my breathing and my heartbeat
are the only sounds I hear.

HEARTPOWER! READER
AMERICAN HEART ASSOCIATION SCHOOLSITE PROGRAM

WHAT IS THE HEART?

by Dr. Alvin & Virginia B. Silverstein

What is the heart? Why is it so important? What does it do in the body?

You probably think you know what the heart looks like. But you probably are wrong. The heart does not look very much like the shapes people draw on Valentine's Day. And it certainly isn't flat, like a paper valentine. A real, live heart is shaped something like an ice-cream cone, with a pointed bottom and a rounded top, like two scoops of ice cream. It is hollow and can fill up with blood. A grown-up's heart is about the size of a fist. It weighs a little less than a pound.

When you pledge allegiance to the flag, you place your hand over the left

Reprinted with permission of Dr. Alvin & Virginia B. Silverstein.

side of your chest. Do you know why? That is supposed to be where the heart is. Actually, the heart is in the middle of the chest. It fits in snugly between the two lungs. But the heart is tipped over, so that there is a little more of it on the left side than on the right. The pointed tip at the bottom of the heart touches the front wall of the chest. Every time the heart beats, it goes *thump* against the chest wall. You can feel the thumps if you press

and again, to form many smaller tubes. These blood vessels carry blood to all parts of the body. The farther from the heart, the more blood vessels there are, and the smaller they are. The tiniest blood vessels, called capillaries, are so small you would need a microscope to see them. Capillaries join to form larger blood vessels. These tubes carry blood back toward the heart. The bigger ones are called veins. The closer to the heart, the fewer the veins there are,

circulatory sys

there with your hand. You can hear them with your ear.

The heart is a pump. Its walls are made of thick muscle. They can squeeze (contract) to send blood rushing out. The blood does not spill all over the place when it leaves the heart. It flows smoothly in tubes called blood vessels.

First the blood flows into tubes called arteries. The arteries that leave the heart are thick tubes. The biggest one, called the aorta, is an inch wide. But the arteries soon branch again

and the larger they are. The largest veins empty blood into the heart.

So the blood vessels of the body carry blood in a circle: moving away from the heart in arteries, traveling to various parts of the body in capillaries, and going back to the heart in veins. Scientists call the heart and blood vessels the circulatory system. They say that blood circulates in the body. And the heart is the important pump that makes this happen.

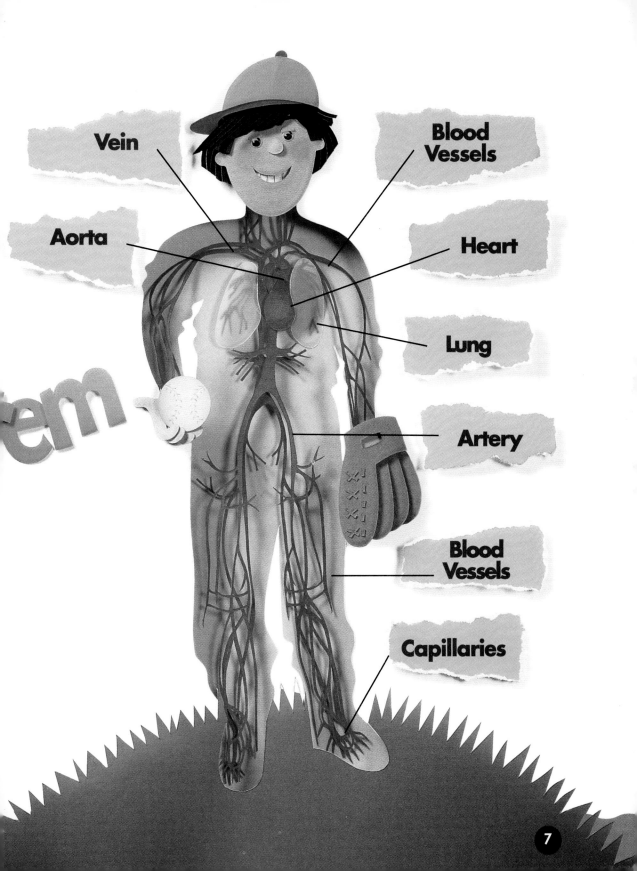

Vein

Blood
Vessels

Aorta

Heart

Lung

em

Artery

Blood
Vessels

Capillaries

7

Eat Healthy Stuff

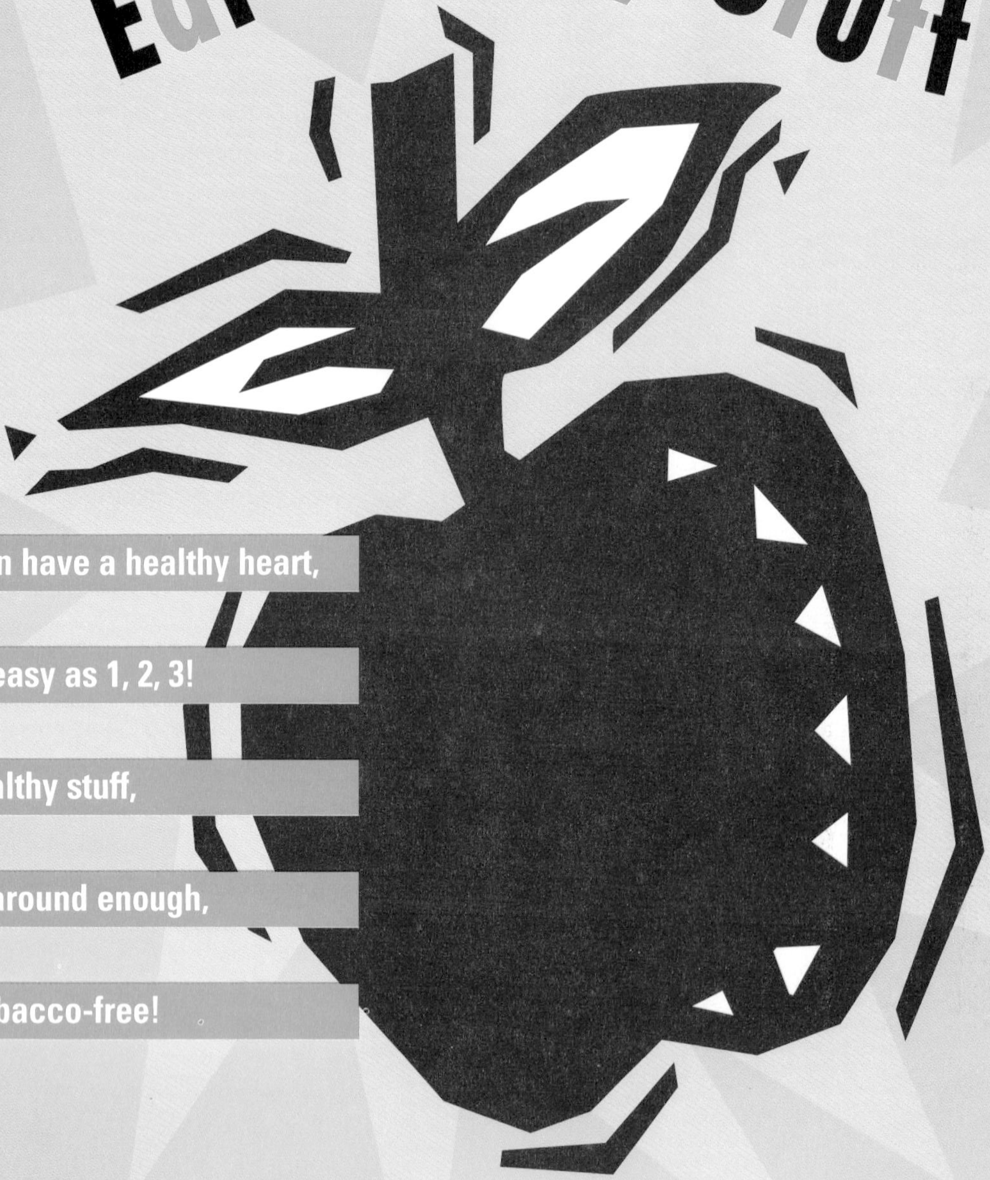

You can have a healthy heart,

It's as easy as 1, 2, 3!

Eat healthy stuff,

Move around enough,

Live tobacco-free!

HEARTPOWER!

The Spratt Family

by Father Gander

Jack Spratt could eat no fat,
His wife could eat no lean.
And so between the two of them,
They licked the platter clean.

Both Spratts, I'm sure of that,
Much better off would be,
To leave the fat upon the plate,
And be cholesterol-free.

Snack Popcorn Attack!

The final bell rings! School's out! What do two out of three kids head for? Snacks. At home, in the vending machine, or at the nearest convenience store. A recent snacking survey asked 1,100 kids in grades three through six about their snacking habits. The kids said that after-school snacking was almost as popular as watching TV.

What are these kids eating? Mostly they're not munching on the healthy snacks they need. Are they secretly eating foods their parents never let them have? Yes. Half the students who had snacks away from home were chowing down on forbidden foods. This is no surprise to kids or parents. They often disagree on what snacks to buy.

Did these kids know what snacks were good for them? The survey found they did. But 46 percent of the kids said taste was the number one reason they liked their favorite snack.

Growing kids need snacks to get enough protein, calories, vitamins, and minerals. Don't think of snacks as "extras." Think of them as mini-meals. Up to 20 percent of daily nutrient needs come from snacks.

After-school snacks let you refuel for the afternoon's activities. So choose those snacks carefully. A "quick fix" candy bar may give you a burst of energy, but it won't last. You'll find yourself in an energy slump before dinner time.

Pick a snack to match your activity. Going in-line skating? Have a small sandwich, a piece of fruit, and milk. The complex carbohydrates will give you energy. The protein, vitamins, and minerals will help you grow and stay healthy. If you plan to watch a movie, go for the pretzels or plain popcorn, or an orange. You may want to avoid getting popcorn at the movie theater,

Dip It!

Everyone loves dips. Take your snacking beyond the ordinary chips and dip. Discover new taste combinations.

Mix and match the dips and dippers listed below.

DIPPERS	DIPS
Fruit slices	Fat-free or low-fat yogurt
Mini rice cakes	Peanut butter
Baked pita chips	Bean dip
Raw veggies	Fat-free salad dressing
Graham crackers	Applesauce
Bread sticks or pretzels	Low-fat cheese spread
Animal crackers	Low-fat pudding

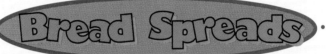

Bread Spreads

BREAD	SPREADS
English muffin	Low-fat cheese spread, canned pear or peach slices
Toasted frozen waffle	Peanut butter
Raisin bread	Low-fat cream cheese and jelly
Pita bread	Peanut butter and thin slices of apple, pear, or banana
Bagel	Low-fat cream cheese and chopped dried fruit
Rice cake	Peanut butter and raisins
Whole-wheat bread	Soft low-fat cream cheese and finely chopped carrots and broccoli
Whole-wheat English muffin	Peanut butter, sliced banana or apple, and honey

For the adventurous, mix and match any of the above to create your own snack treat.

though. Some movie theater popcorn is extremely high in fat.

Grazing Through the Day

Snacking has become a way of life for many busy families. Americans spend $13.4 billion a year on snack foods. Today's busy schedules often don't leave time for a traditional meal. A new eating trend is called "grazing." People who graze eat many mini-meals during the day. Recent studies have found that there may be some health benefits to grazing. Of course, that depends on what foods you graze on.

In one study, people who ate several mini-meals had lower cholesterol levels. Snacks also keep you from getting so hungry that you overeat at your next meal.

Pyramid of Snacks

Make snacks work for you. Smart snacking helps you get the protein, carbohydrates, vitamins, and minerals you need every day. The snacking pyramid below shows how snacks fit into the Food Guide Pyramid.

Think Before You Snack

Bite-size crackers and cookies are fun snacks, but it's easy to forget how much you've eaten. Instead of eating them straight from the box, put some in a bowl.

Beware the "fat-free" snacks. Fat-free does NOT mean eat as much as you want. It's OK to treat yourself to fat-free cookies and desserts once in a while. Just remember, they may be high in sugar. Also, they give you few vitamins and minerals.

C
Chip

Skim Mil
Low-fat Chees
Low-fat Yogur
Low-fat Frozen Yogur

Fresh Fruit   Fruit Juic
Frozen Fruit Bars   Dried Frui

Bread   Cereal   Low-fat Cracker
Pita   Pretzels   Low-fat Muffins   Plain

SNACKING

HEARTPOWER! READER
AMERICAN HEART ASSOCIATION SCHOOLSITE PROGRAM

There's nothing wrong with having sweets occasionally. Try pairing them up with a healthy snack. For example, cookies with low-fat frozen yogurt, angel food cake with fresh berries, or some chocolate chips in your cereal snack mix.

Creative Snacking

Cereal Crunchies: Mix your favorite cereal with dried fruit bits, raisins, and pretzels. Challenge your taste buds by using two or three cereals instead of just one. Experiment with combining different flavors.

Popcorn Munchies: Mix together plain popcorn, dry-roasted peanuts, raisins, and dried fruit bits.

Spicy Popcorn: Add zip to plain popcorn. Sprinkle on flavors such as chili powder, garlic powder, onion powder, or soy sauce.

Snackateria

Set up a "snackateria" for a party or whenever friends are over. This is a great group activity. You will need:

▲ Fresh fruit and veggies cut into bite-size pieces. Examples: apples, pears, carrots, cucumber, broccoli, zucchini, green pepper

▲ Bite-size cubes of low-fat cheese. Examples: American, Swiss, cheddar

▲ Long toothpicks or small skewers

Let everyone make their own kabobs: all fruit, all veggies, all cheese, or all mixed up! Have a contest for the best-tasting, best-looking, or strangest combination.

Interested in more snack recipes? Check the school or public library for kids' cookbooks. You'll find making snacks can be almost as much fun as eating them.

okies

Nuts
Lean Deli Meat
Peanut Butter
Bean Dip

Salad   Vegetable Soup
Raw Veggies   Vegetable Juice

agels   Corn Tortillas   English Muffins
corn   Rice Cakes   Bread Sticks   Waffles

PYRAMID

This is called your resting heart rate. The faster your heart returns to normal, the better it is for your heart. The more you exercise, the quicker your heart rate will return to its resting rate.

To really help your heart get stronger, you need at least 30 minutes of *aerobic* (ər ō´ bik; exercise that conditions the heart and lungs) exercise three to four times a week. This means that you need to get your heart beating faster than normal and keep it beating faster for at least 30 minutes. So, how do you do that? You start by getting off the couch and moving. Any kind of moving will help. You can in-line skate, jog, hike, bike, or swim. Get a friend to get fit with you. How about joining a soccer team, or basketball? You can sign up for a dance class, gymnastics, tennis, or track. You can do something as simple as mowing your lawn or taking your dog for a brisk walk. He needs exercise, too!

Work Those Muscles

Taking care of your heart is a great reason to exercise, but there are other good reasons, too. Keeping fit improves the strength of your bones, muscles, and joints. Those with stronger muscles usually sit, stand, and walk with better *posture* (pos´chər; the position of the body). Good posture makes you look healthier and more attractive. To make your muscles stronger, you need to work them. For instance, climbing and bicycling strengthen your leg muscles. Pull-ups and push-ups help to strengthen your arms, and sit-ups help to strengthen your stomach muscles.

It Feels Good

So you still have to sit in front of the TV for your favorite show? Why not spend that time stretching your muscles? Stretching helps you to be more *flexible* (flek′ sə bəl; able to bend without breaking). Stretch your arms, legs, back, stomach, and neck. Do it slowly, without jerking. It is good for your muscles, and helps you to relax.

Get your whole family to join in and have a family fitness stretch and strengthen night. Do some sit-ups together. Do some easy exercises together, like marching in place. Take turns being the exercise leader. What's important is that you aren't just sitting there. And remember: Always warm up before and after exercising.

Now that you know why you need to be fit and how to be fit, go find a friend to get fit with. Remember these steps to fitness: warm-up, aerobics, muscle strengthening, flexibility, and stretching. So, make a deal with your friend to turn off the tube, and get energized with exercise.

Why Should

GOOD LOOKING

Everybody wants to look good. When you are fit, you look and feel great!

BREATHE EASILY

We all have to breathe to live. Regular exercise means it's easier for your body to get all the oxygen (air) it needs to perform well.

CIRCULATE YOUR BLOOD AROUND

Your heart has to pump your blood all around your body. The cleaner the pathways, or blood vessels, are, the better blood can circulate. People who exercise don't have as many fatty deposits in their blood vessels to block the flow of blood.

I Exercise?

FIRM, NOT FLABBY

When you're fit, you won't have many layers of fatty tissue under your skin.

YOUR HEARTBEAT

Your heart is the most important muscle in your body. It has to pump the blood all around your body—from your toes to your nose. And that's an important job.

Exercise makes your heart stronger. A stronger heart doesn't have to work as hard as a weak heart.

Think of a car. If you make your car work too hard for a long time, it will fall apart. If you keep it well-oiled and repaired, it runs smoothly and lasts longer.

A stronger heart lasts longer!

WHO INVENTED RUNNING?

BY PETE GARVEY

Cave men invented running
Three million years ago.
They ran away from lions, tigers,
Bears, and buffalo.
'Cause if cave people DIDN'T run
(Just stood around in bunches)
All sorts of hungry animals
Would have them for their lunches!
Today we don't need animals
To make us want to run.
We do it 'cause it keeps us fit.
Besides all that, it's FUN!

HEARTPOWER! READER
AMERICAN HEART ASSOCIATION SCHOOLSITE PROGRAM

Live Tobacco-Free

You can have a healthy heart,

It's as easy as 1, 2, 3!

Eat healthy stuff,

Move around enough,

Live tobacco-free!

HEARTPOWER! SM

No Ifs, Ands or

by Lisa Feder-Feitel

Look around you. It may seem like a lot of kids smoke. It sure looked that way to 10-year-old Kyle Salling. "When I went to an amusement park near my home," he said, "I saw kids a little older than me hanging out in big groups, smoking."

Lots of kids do light up. In fact, every day, 3,000 kids smoke a cigarette for the first time. As many as half of them will go on to smoke cigarettes daily. And over time, they may join the nearly 450,000 Americans who die each year from smoking-related illnesses.

That's got many folks upset. The Food and Drug Administration says nicotine-filled cigarettes are a harmful, addicting drug—like cocaine or heroin. The FDA wants smokes to be

Seventy-seven percent of all smokers want to quit, but can't because of nicotine addiction.

are addicting. And some kids, like Sean Hutchinson, 11, agree.

"Kids think that one smoke can't hurt them. Then they try another and another," he says. "Pretty soon they get addicted—and then they don't have a choice anymore."

Some Good News

The good news is that most kids from 10 to 18 don't smoke. And

considered in the same way as those drugs.

Joycelyn Elders, a former U.S. Surgeon General, agrees. "When cigarettes were first used, we didn't know that they could cause cancer," she says. "I'm sure if cigarettes were introduced today—with all that we know about them—we would never allow them to be sold.

"Nicotine is addictive," adds Dr. Elders. That means that once your body becomes used to it, it needs and wants more nicotine. Dr. Elders worries that some young people still don't know cigarettes

Nicotine, an ingredient found in cigarettes, is as addictive as the drug heroin.

according to one report, seven out of every 10 high school seniors think smoking is a dirty habit. These kids say they won't date a smoker.

The report also shows that if most

Up in Smoke

According to *The Surgeon General's Report for Kids About Smoking*, the average smoker spends about $700 a year on cigarettes. Here's what you could do with all that money:

- Play 2,800 video games.

- Take 40 friends to the movies, then order 19 pizzas (with everything) to eat while you're reading your 162 new comic books.

- Talk on the phone to your friend in another state for 126 hours, 22 minutes.

- Buy 1,400 seedlings to plant three acres of oak, hickory, walnut, or ash trees.

- Save it in a bank. At 5% interest, you'd have more than $25,000 after 20 years.

No Joke, Joe: Joe Camel is part of a cigarette advertising campaign. Some people have attacked these ads, saying they are aimed at kids. The makers of Camel cigarettes say that's not true.

kids don't start smoking during their school years, they probably will never smoke at all. In fact, 60 percent of today's smokers started using cigarettes by the age of 13.

Right now, the U.S. Congress hopes to outlaw smoking in schools, youth centers, and other public places where kids spend time. One reason: Smoking is especially dangerous to kids, because their lungs are still growing. Kids exposed to even secondhand smoke—smoke from other people's cigarettes—can get coughs, sore throats, and serious lung diseases.

More Help

Private companies are also getting on the no-smoking bandwagon. McDonald's outlawed smoking in its restaurants. Airlines, buses, and taxis are mostly smoke-free, as well as some major-league sports stadiums. Yet kids continue to start a habit that can be deadly. How come? "I think they feel cool because they're part of a group," says Kyle Salling, of Cincinnati, Ohio. "They think it will get them more friends."

Nine-year-old Emily Sweeney from Ventnor, N.J., says, "I think kids start to smoke because their friends pressure them." Adds Emily, "When a friend asks if you want a cigarette, it can be hard to say no."

Making or keeping friends isn't the only reason kids start lighting up, points out Adam Tabor, nine, from New Iberia, La. "Kids sometimes

There is a radioactive substance in cigarettes. Smoking a pack a day for 10 years exposes you to the same amount of radiation as 200 chest X-rays.

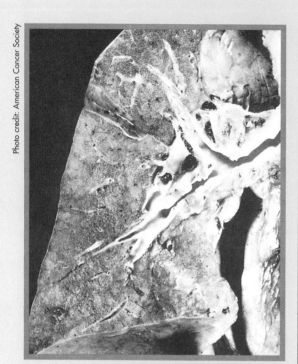

Photo credit: American Cancer Society

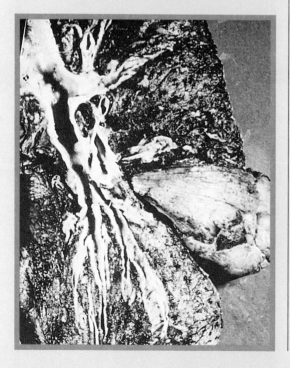

start to smoke because their parents do," he says. "They think it's all right to do it because their parents do it."

Sean Hutchinson thinks kids smoke out of boredom. "They smoke because they don't have anything else to do," says the 11-year-old from Fort Smith, Ark. "But kids can't see the harm smoking does to their friends, because most of the damage is inside their bodies."

For some kids, deciding whether or not to smoke is a tough choice. But the answer is clear to Kyle Salling. "In our school," he says, "we looked at a model of the lungs of a smoker. They were black and gooey and gross. If kids could see that black lung just once, that would do it for them. No kids would want to hurt themselves like that."

The photo at top left shows a section of a healthy lung. Below it is part of a lung from a smoker. It was damaged by a disease called emphysema, which makes breathing very difficult. This deadly disease was brought on by smoking.

It's a Lungful

ACETANISOLE, ACETIC ACID, ACETOIN, ACETOPHENONE, 6-ACETOXYDIHYDROTHEASPIRANE, 2ACETYL-3ETHYLPYRAZINE, 2-ACETYL-5-METHYLFURAN, ACETYLPYRAZINE, 2-ACETYLPYRIDINE, 3-ACETYLPYRIDINE, 2-ACETYLHIAZOLE, ACONITIC ACID, di-ALANINE, ALLYL HEXANOATE, ALLYL IONONE, AMMONIA, AMMONIUM BICARBONATE, AMMONIUM HYDROXIDE, AMMONIUM PHOSPHAGE DIBASIC, AMMONIUM SULFIDE, AMYL ALCOHOL, AMYL BUTRATE, AMYL FORMATE, AMYL OCTANOATE, alpha-AMYLCIN-NAMALDEHYDE, trans-ANETHOLE, ANISYL ACETATE, ANISYL ALCOHOL, ANISYL FORMATE, ANISYL PHENYLACETATE, l-ARGININE, ASAFETIDA FLUID, l-ASPARAGINE MONOHYDRATE, l-ASPARTIC ACID, BALSAM PERU, BENZALDEHYDE, ABENZALDEHYDE GLYCERYL ACETAL, BENZOIC ACID, BENZOIN, BENZOIN RESIN, BENZOPHENONE, BENZYL ALCOHOL, BENZYL BENZOATE, BENZYL BUTYRATE, BENZYL CINNAMATE, BENZYL PROPIONATE, BENZYL SALICYLATE, BISABOLENE, BORNYL ACETATE, BUCHU LEAF OIL, l,3-BUTANEDIOL, 2,3-BUTANEDIONE, l-BUTANOL, 2-BUTANONE, 4(2-BUTENYLIDENE)-3, BUTYL ACETATE, BUTYL BUTYRATE, BUTYL BUTYRYL LACTATE, BUTYL ISOVALERATE, BUTYL PHENYLACETATE, BUTYL UNDECYLENATE, 3-BUTYLIDENEPHTHALIDE, BUTYRIC ACID, CADINENE, CALCIUM CARBONATE, CAMPHENE, CANANGA OIL, CAPSICUM OLEORESIN, CARVACROL, 4-CARVOMENTHENOL, l-CARVONE, beta-CARYOPHYLLENE, beta-CARYOPHYLLENE OXIDE, CASTOREUM, CEDROL, CINNAMALDEHYDE, CINNAMIC ACID, CINNAMYL ACETATE, CINNAMYL ALCOHOL, CINNAMYL ISOVALERATE, CINNAMYL PROPIONATE, CIRAL, CITRONELLYL BUTYRATE, CITRONELLYL ISOBUTYRATE, CIVET ABSOLUTE, CUMINALDEHYDE, para-CYMENE, l-CYSTEINE, DECADIENAL, delta-DECALACTONE, gamma-DECALATONE, DECANAL, DECANOIC ACID, l-DECANOL, 2-DECENAL, DEHYDROMENTHOFUROLACTONE, DIETHYL MALONATE, DIETHYL SEBACATE, 2,3-DIETHYLPYRAZINE, DIHYDRO ANETHOLE, 5,7-DIHYDRO-2-METHYLTHIENO (3,4-D) PYRIMIDINE, meta-DIMETHOXYBENZENE, para-DIMETHOXYBENZENE, 2,6-DIMETHOXYPHENOL DIONE, 3,5-DIMETHYL-1,2-CYCLOPENTANEDIONE, 3,7-DIMETHYL-1,3,6-OCTATRIENE, 4,5-DIMETHYL-3-HYDROXY-2,5-DIHYDROFURAN-2-ONE, 6,10-DIMETHYL-6-OCTENOIC ACID, 2,4-DIMETHYLACETOPHENONE, DIMETHYLBENZYL ALCOHOL, alpha-DIMETHYLPHENETHYL ACETATE, alpha-DIMETHYLPHENETHYL BUTYRATE, 2,3-DIMETHYLPYRAZINE, 2,5-DIMETHYLPYRAZINE, 2,6-DIMETHYLPYRAZINE, DIMETHYLTETRAHYDROBENZOFURANONE, delta-DODECALACTONE, gamma-DODECALACTONE, para-ETHOXYBENZALDEHYDE, ETHYL 10-UNDECENOATE, EHTYL 2-METHYLBUTYRATE, ETHYL ACETATE, ETHYL ACETOACETATE, ETHYL ALCOHOL, ETHYL BENZOATE, ETHYL BUTYRATE, ETHYL CINNAMATE, ETHYL DECANOATE, ETHYL FENCHOL, EHTYL FUROATE, ETHYL HEPTANOATE, ETHYL HEXANOATE, ETHYL ISOVALERATE, ETHYL LACTATE, ETHYL LAURATE, ETHYL LEVULINATE, ETHYL MALTOL, ETHYL METHYL PHENYLGLYCIDATE, ETHYL MYRISTATE, ETHYL NONANOATE, ETHYL OCTADECANOATE, ETHYL OCTANOATE, ETHYL OLEATE, ETHYL PALMITATE, ETHYL PHENYLACETATE, ETHYL PROPIONATE, ETHYL SALICYLATE, ETHYL trans-2-BUTENOATE, ETHYL VALERATE, ETHYL VANILLIN, 2-ETHYL(OR METHYL)-(3,5 and 6) METHOXYPYRAZINE, 2-ETHYL-1-HEXANOL, 3-ETHYL-2-HYDROXY-2-CYCLOPENTEN-1-ONE, 2-ETHYL-3, (5 OR 6)-DIMETHYLRAZINE, 5-ETHYL-3-HYDROXY-4-METHYL-2(5H)-FURANONE, 2-ETHYL-3-METHYLPYRAZINE, 4-ETHYLBENZALDEHYDE, 4-ETHYLGUAIACOL, para-ETHYLPHENOL, 3-ETHYLPYRIDINE, FURFURYL MERCAPTAN, 4-(2-FURYL)-3-BUTEN-2-ONE, GENET ABSOLUTE, GERANIOL, GERANYL ACETATE, GERANYL BUTYRATE, GERANYL FORMATE, GERANYL ISOVALERATE, GERANYL PHENYLACETATE, GLYCEROL, GLYCYRRHIZIN AMMONIATED, GUAIACOL, 2,4-HEPTADIENAL, gamma-HEPTALACTONE, HEPTANOIC ACID, 2-HEPTANONE, 3-HEPTEN-2-ONE, 2-HEPTEN-4-ONE, 4-HEPTENAL, trans-2-HEPTENAL, HEPTYL ACETATE, omega-6-HEXADECENLACTONE, gamma-HEXALACTONE, HEXANAL, HEXANOIC ACID, 2-HEXEN-1-OL, 3-HEXEN-1-OL, cis-3-HEXEN-1-YL-ACETATE, 2-HEXENAL, 3-HEXANOIC ACID, trans-2-HEXENOIC ACID, cis-3-HEXENYL FORMATE, HEXYL 2-METHYLBUTYRATE, HEXYL ACETATE, HEXYL ALCOHOL, HEXYL PHENYLACETATE, 1-HISTIDINE, 5-HYDROX-2,4-DECADIENOIC ACID delta-LACTONE, 4-HYDROXY-2,5-DIMETHYL-3(2H)-FURANONE, 2-HYDROXY-3,5,5-TRIMETHYL-2-CYCLOHEXEN-1-ONE, 4-HYDROXY-3-PENTENOIC ACID LACTONE, 2-HYDROXY-4-METHYLBENZALDEHYDE, 4-HYDROXYBUTANOIC ACID LACTNE, HYDROXYCITRONELLAL, 6-HYDROXYDIHYDROTHEASPIRANE, 4-(para-HYDROXYPHENYL)-2-BUTANONE, HYSSOP OIL, IMMORTELLE ABSOLUTE, alpha-IONONE, beta-IONONE, alpha-IRONE, ISOAMYL ACETATE, ISOAMYL BENZOATE, ISOAMYL BUTYRATE, ISOAMYL CINNAMATE, ISOAMYL FORMATE, ISOAMYL HEXANOATE, ISOAMYL ISOVALERATE, ISOAMYL OCTANOATE, ISOAMYL PHENYLACETATE, PROPENYLGUAETHOL, SKATOLE, 1,5,5,9-TETRAMETHYL-13-OXATRICYCLO (8.3.0.0) (4,9)TRIDECANE-FEMA GRAS, VALERALDEHYDE, UNDECANAL, UREA,

There are 599 ingredients that are added to tobacco in the making of cigarettes. We've listed only about 225 of those ingredients, which people inhale every time they light up.

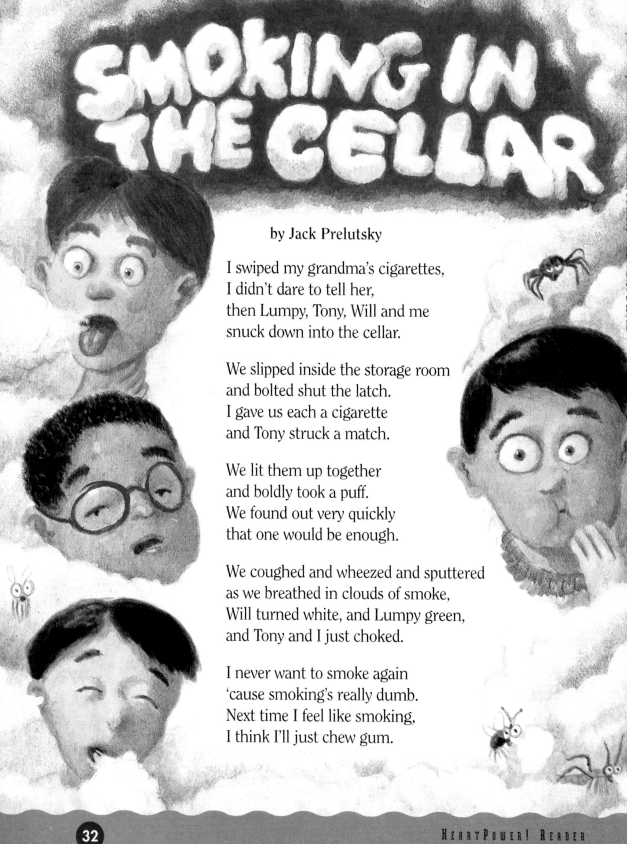

SMOKING IN THE CELLAR

by Jack Prelutsky

I swiped my grandma's cigarettes,
I didn't dare to tell her,
then Lumpy, Tony, Will and me
snuck down into the cellar.

We slipped inside the storage room
and bolted shut the latch.
I gave us each a cigarette
and Tony struck a match.

We lit them up together
and boldly took a puff.
We found out very quickly
that one would be enough.

We coughed and wheezed and sputtered
as we breathed in clouds of smoke,
Will turned white, and Lumpy green,
and Tony and I just choked.

I never want to smoke again
'cause smoking's really dumb.
Next time I feel like smoking,
I think I'll just chew gum.